Spectral Realms

No. 23 ‡ Summer 2025

Edited by S. T. Joshi

The spectral realms that thou canst see
With eyes veil'd from the world and me.

H. P. LOVECRAFT, "To a Dreamer"

SPECTRAL REALMS is published twice a year by Hippocampus Press,
P.O. Box 641, New York, NY 10156 (www.hippocampuspress.com).
Copyright © 2025 by Hippocampus Press.
All works are copyright © 2025 by their respective authors.
Cover art and design by Daniel V. Sauer.
Hippocampus Press logo by Anastasia Damianakos.

ISBN 978-1-61498-473-3   ISSN 2333-4215

Contents

Poems

Stand Not in My Shadow

Manuel Pérez-Campos

I am a barbarian king abominable to the solar
order: the long night of insentience
which persecutes me in sleep until I fidget
grudgingly—and growl—seeks release in this foetid
campus belli at the edge of time where
the fortress of the lotus-eating necromancers
issues its edicts of doom by coursing through
my indefatigable arm to clang down the hilt
of a truculence-guided sword on the helmet
of my confronter so as to pierce his visage
with shards from his fragmented skull: the squirting
blood of the nimbus-murked fallen I stoop
to drink: and roar my berserkers forward:
unenvied by my spiked collar mastiffs, I advance:
soon the gates of the fortress shall be ripped
apart: and the beleaguered necromancers in their creepy
self-indulgent robes, bereft of a phalanx
to insure their continuance, shall be eaten
raw by us in breechclout while still alive.

Dedicated to the memory of Robert E. Howard

The Land of the Stolen Children

David Schembri

The pale ones drank their forbidden rum
As they scurried over lands of stone;
When dark clouds formed to shield the sun,
Their sights would pierce through skin and bone.

My daughter lay upon a bed of straw,
Wrapped in a rug sewn with red;
I guarded the window till my eyes grew sore
In those misty lands of the dead.

This is a tale that would pain your heart,
Inked on parchments torn and true.
When darkness comes, the nightmare will start,
With fangs so vast, they'll run you through.

Plucked from their beds, one by one,
Children were stolen into the night,
To be turned into those that fear the sun,
Their eyes veined red, their skin so white.

I tired of being a slave
To the ghastly terrors that dwell around;
I cradled my girl, whom I longed to save,
Kissing her forehead and setting her down.

With a necklace of garlic and wooden cross
I dared to pass the village gate;
Stepping over rocks of wilted moss,
I ventured out to test my fate.

With a loaded musket I pushed my search
Through the tunnels of the forest, diving deep.
In the dark hollows within trees of birch,
The burrow appeared where the pale ones sleep.

I scattered my trap in that dark, dead place,
Tossing gunpowder here and there;
In the tree tops I hid, with frost on my face,
I prayed and longed for fate to be fair.

Time slipped by—was it minutes or hours?
Creatures emerged out from the dark.
My musket, it fired, forming smoky towers;
I rejoiced as my bullet found its mark.

Their howls screeched within the fire's embrace.
I ran through the woods from the burning wake,
My heart, it pounded at a violent pace
As the heat followed me like a monstrous snake.

I woke the town crying, "Hell has come near!"
As the forest's glow rose higher and higher,
Everyone filled a pail and formed a frontier
To fight in the hope the flames would retire.

Come morning Hell's mouth did not lick our gate.
As we'd drenched our borders from east to west,
The heat and smoke retreated before late,
And our stolen children were finally put to rest.

Long Hence

F. J. Bergmann

Some of us refuse to admit that we are dead,
won't speak of *changing*; prefer to say, instead,
that we've evolved, improved, acquired . . . well,
some altered tastes. Hounded, outlawed, we fled
our human families after . . . We won't dwell
upon unfortunate . . . incidents that sped
us into other company. What was mine,
now *ours*: those few who dare the wood
by night-tide, their flesh-scent sweet as wine,
become mere vessels brimming with warm blood
for our delectation. Ages ago
we learned what risen moons compel to wring.
Between the shadowy trees, a fire's glow.
We crouch upon our haunches, tense to spring.

A bout-rimé from "Aftermath" by Willa Cather

A Giant of the Future

Maxwell I. Gold

At the cold, empty edge of oblivion, I saw that grotesque, hideous mass towering over the world. Unbelievably decadent, coated with slime and putrid ruins that once were cities; along its skin dotted by monuments forged by a race, forgotten in name, their memory a corpse dripped from every pustule orifice of that giant thing. Lumbering ever slowly through time, reason contorted by the giant's twisted frame, smashed both physical and unknowable spaces beneath its colossal steps with great indifference.

The awakening was inevitable. Arrested from a slumber thought to be eternal, I knew the Giant would come for us all, the Future's foul harbinger. Soon there was nothing left, trapped and subsumed by the beast's pale, oleaginous skin; oil then replaced water, metal for the trees, fire swallowed the clouds, and yet after death had its gluttonous share, there seemed to be no end in sight. Not all at once, the ground ceased its tremendous quivers, whereupon silence overcame the deathful atmosphere that had seized an already broken world, composed of gruesome visions and dreadful music. And I stood at the feet of that thing, in the shadow of creature so splendid and grim, whose monstrous shape, while familiar, filled me with a deep abhorrence for the present, so I welcomed it—I welcomed the end, The Future.

Ys

J. G. Maybrook

Except in dreams, what once was there
Is lost to us beyond repair;
The Blessed Realm has ceased to be:
Gone is the palace by the sea,
And gone the meadows once so fair.

The awful wave, it did not spare
The kingdom sleeping unaware,
So taking it from you and me
    Except in dreams.

When in my dreams I see it there,
A place beyond the world's compare,
I sigh for what is lost to me
Forevermore beneath the sea:
I will not find it anywhere
    Except in dreams.

Through Iridescent Caves

Andrew White

Across the rainbow in shimmering waves
Through fields of stars and ashes,
Moonlight shines and the ocean crashes—
She walks through iridescent caves.
Radiant energy betrays the dark,
And resident ghouls refuse to attack.
She glides through the depths, a picture in black,
The horrors held at bay by her luminous spark.
Rán smiles on her at the end of the road.
She bows and takes in her glittering abode.

Red Thoughts

Simon MacCulloch

I will fall through the empty sky of her stare
To the pit that her shark teeth rim,
And I'll boil in the laughter bubbling there
Where the souls of her old loves swim
In the ebb and the surge of her whim.

My remains will hunt as a brittle husk
Through the halls of her castle-crypt,
Like a dog on the scent of the bitter musk
That the dream of her smile once dripped
On the heart that her red claws ripped.

Then I'll lay my skull on an altar-stone
Where a goat-faced priest presides,
And he'll stir the slime in the sphere of bone
Where the germ of my passion hides,
And I'll die, but the germ abides.

So soon you will watch as the stars are obscured
By the smoke as the hellfire catches,
And the oven heats red for the red thoughts lured
To this castle of heaven-made matches,
Till the egg of the lamia hatches.

Streetwalker as Stalker

LindaAnn LoSchiavo

"The moon, with its pale glow, casts a mysterious spell upon the world,
awakening the beast within."—Gary Brandner, "The Howling" (1977)

The cigarette's a prop, badass glamour.
Strategically ripped fishnet stockings
Suggest my needs will make it easier
To offer less, avoid the condom fuss.

A man's assessment of a harlot's heart
Includes how high those heels, how tight her skirt.

A goth chick seems sufficiently sin-dipped,
Equipped for kinky sex, coded darkness,
Unlikely to snuff out slow-stroked smolder.

He won't suspect this is my time of month—
Bright full moon cameoing snout and claws
That pin him to the bed, unleash his blood,
Ripping apart his flesh till sucked bone dry.

Nightsong

Lee Clark Zumpe

She waltzes across the threshold,
gazing dazedly with twilight-tinted eyes—
each contemptuous glance
distorting fragments of the
dying day.

Her breath is heavy with
soft sighs and vespertine whispers—
a secret, sensuous language
too eloquent to be uttered
outside shadowed alcoves.

She scowls darkly as she crosses,
each sharp frown an assault—
her instinct and unyielding tenacity
splinters the fleeing sunlight
into scattered shards.

She descends the gloamy stairway,
negotiating familiar stygian lairs—
detaching herself from the sanctuary
of melancholic prayer
and the luxury of dream.

Death-Palace

Benjamin Blake

In the death-palace
The trees are waking up,
And something stalks the length of the colonnade
As quiet as a nighttime cat.

In the death-palace
Inverted torches burn eternal,
And ivy chokes infants
Who never breathed their first
Yet alone their last.

In the death-palace
Canines sit forever silent in contemplative vigil,
And forgotten names are whispered
To stoic angels
With downcast eyes.

In the death-palace
The resurrection men caress with avaricious hands,
Offer entrails in which to foretell the future.

In the death-palace
You are being called home
To the death-palace,
To the death-palace.

The Monster Regrets

Adele Gardner

"I didn't mean to hurt you." That's the short version,
The catchphrase, my only way to your heart.
It's true, I didn't know my own strength.
I didn't know you thought it was unforgivable
For me to kill that guy who disrespected you
By saying the shake machine was broken, then
Giving you a burger when you wanted wings.
I thought you'd appreciate my loyalty, my concern,
The way I wanted to feed you what you liked best.
After all, you praised the cat who brought you voles.
I have to admit, I was angry when you yelled at me.
I never want to get angry with you.
Having the strength of a monster is not so easy
In this fragile mortal world where bones snap
At barely a thought. What you don't know:
Your red, shouting face and teary eyes
Hurt me more than dropping a mountain on me
Or sending a sky full of lightning I could swat away like flies.
Those things don't matter. But your regard—
That's my life's blood. That's why I'm here.
I'm your friend, and when you want to run away
It feels like razors down my spine, like the burning manacles
The gods snapped on my wrists when they first captured me.
They didn't understand: death is only a doorway.
I'll get back to you, whatever they might do.
You might do well to remember that, darling.

Resurrection Song

Wade German

How strange is the silence through heaven—
    But stranger the sound of the horns
Which sunder the silence with soundings,
    A summons, or signal that warns:

The mountains now tremble and crumble,
    The earth is uplifted and heaves;
All rivers and oceans are emptied,
    The warp of the world now unweaves:

The tombstones and monuments topple
    As emptiness under them yawns;
Green limbs from the earth come up groping—
    The dead are arisen at dawn!

They shamble in semblance of walking,
    They stumble and utter odd cries;
They gaze with the gaze of the mindless,
    With dust of decay in their eyes . . .

The Earth is now finally peaceful,
    All kingdoms delivered from strife:
The Kingdom has come with strange feasters
    To feast at the supper of Life!

Bluebeard's Donjon

Manuel Arenas

In Bluebeard's donjon skulk the shades of wives whom he has killed.
Abiding mid the tacky muck of blood which he has spilled.
Their broken bodies hang on hooks about the dreadful room,
To warn the errant sister-wife of their impending doom.
A fairy key unlocks the door to this ensanguined lair.
But enter thus at your own risk, if you should find you dare.
Don't let slip that accurst key from out your dainty hand.
For if upon the clotted gore it should befall to land,
A smirch of guilt will then appear, to mark the rash trespass
Betokening a grim sentence that one may not bypass
To join th' horrific harem trapped within this torture-tomb
And forewarn the next ingénue that sneaks into the room.

Wind Phone Callback

Ann K. Schwader

A booth is better for restraining words
too rare for air. This disconnected line
connects enough: left silent by design,
the handset beckons memories interred
alive. Like moths to bonfires, only spurred
by death, they immolate themselves to fine
& painless ash. To closure as resigned
amnesia. Don't consider those who heard
too slowly to respond from underground
before the call went cold. If their replies
might dare to contradict survivors, bringing
disquiet home, so what? Ignore the sound
that rises now through midnight autumn skies
persistent as a whisper. One phone ringing.

The Silence

Livia E. De Souza

My world was still: quiet as I had never known it to be. The spectral hand clasped me, though this proffered grip had moved from my palm to my throat. Its promise and my assent had been enough.

It entwined itself with my being: commanding when I would relent, striking when I would retreat. Through muscle and sharpened steel, it conducted my brutal revenge, and I was plunged into a world of silence.

Silence, but for the swinging and whining of the ceiling fan in its socket. Silence, but for this persistent thrumming that had gone unnoticed, held beneath the ruthless tide of growled, caustic words.

Yet those words were no more. The cords which birthed them had slackened and stilled, their fleshy reliquary enshrined in a spreading, shimmering crimson font.

My hands were still freshly wet from their grim baptism.

Cheap smoke filled my lungs, and liquor heated my throat. My unseen guide had uncoiled in a breath, its glimmering essence disentangling from my nerves.

And I had gladly accepted the offer of this haunted salvation: the silence of my kingdom.

To Sobek

Dmitri Akers

The seeds of sin, this reptile eye may hold,
Are tears that roll and dampen scales and wiles;
What love or joy is this? His eyes may roll
To see a scene of death: a beast defiles
The soul of joy itself—as prey are drowned
For Sobek's hungry rage, for watery graves,
To bleed a life of blood, to whet his glaive,
His ruddy seeds are borne within the ground!
O Sobek! Crocodile and God of lust
Thy seed may seep from every corpse's mouth,
Thy seeds are blown along a wind from South.
For Sobek's seeds are fertile wheat to dust,
A murrain's rust, a scythe—as babies cried,
A soul incised, with pairs of eyeballs pried . . .

End of Days

William Clunie

You wander on this spectral plain,
together with the other wraiths,
schlepping to the charnel pit
yonder past the flensery.

They take your skin before you're far.
Bones rattle in your absent ears.
The eyes they left behind shed tears,
but that will pass as sorrow fades

like flowers clad in monochrome
along a path no longer trod.

Shadow Play

Ngo Anh Binh Khoa

My wife has not been herself as of late,
Her face a pallid mask whose warmth of old
Has faded, and what's left is but a cold
And quiet ghost trapped in a trance-like state.

Since that lame cat she took in disappeared
(That vile and vicious black-furred parasite!),
My wife has often screamed its name at night
And, sobbing, muttered things I could not hear.

Though I have tried to soothe her bursts of pain,
She's lost more weight and spurned the food I cook.
Now, gaunt and ghoulish is her wounded look;
New scratch marks mar her bloodied skin again.

 By day she stays locked in her lightless room,
But her strange footsteps haunt the house at night;
Her stumbling heels would dodge my line of sight
Till dawn arrives, and silence once more looms.

My plans to catch her have been all for naught
For days, but I've grown more familiar
With her set patterns. Now I've cornered her
And seen the dead rat her stained teeth have caught.

I stare as she grins and falls to the ground,
Unmoving, like a puppet with cut strings;
From out her shadow then, a large shape springs—
Her lost black cat! It flees with cackling sounds!
By my wife's bloodless corpse, my scream resounds.

For the Nightmuse

Scott J. Couturier

Nightmuse—
To You I dedicate this script.
No other spirit has from my head
Torn such otherworldly visions
Of wonder & horror, awe & dread.

Spawn of somber chasms where
Entities unspeakable writhe,
& eyes of evilest intent stare,
From their mortal sockets ripped;

Unholiest of holies, sacrosanct,
Blasphemous unction, balm & bale.
Taste of rotten honey & myrrh
Anoints my tongue as tapers fail.

Nightmuse—
Divine darkness robed in light,
Scion of forsaken planets & stars,
Keeper of twinned terror & delight:
Answerer of any question asked.

From dream you bleed into being,
Invade & inspire, possess & enchant.
On midnight winds you whisper;
On grave's exhalation you incant.

Asphodel of regretful remembrance,
River of thirst, rilling chillest fear;
Mephitis of bliss, monstrous semblance,
Solemn & Stygian idol of Weir.

Nightmuse—
To You I dedicate this script,
Dictated by your angel of despair.
Wings like shrouds enfold my eyes
As mantic incense invades the air,
All senses now & forever stripped:

For "Fair is foul, & foul is fair."

The Withers

Lori R. Lopez

They may give you the jitters, the deplorable twitters,
their smiles snicky-snacky, their cusps clicky-clacky.
So bent and misshapen, all noxious and scrapen
from the bottom of the barrel in outdated apparel,
with manners misplacen, quite terribly disgracen,
ahunching and crunching, four heads all abunching.
Grimy and kerblimy, most soft and awful-slimy,
a quartet of dun-keepers; the snarliest sleepers . . .
watch out for the Withers or suffer much dithers!

Conspiracy-hatched, their rooftops are thatched
by black and yellow furs the consistency of burrs
that can stick to the skin or the strands they sleep in—
tying ends, weaving tangles, twisting dense mangles,
till the mane's all a knot. They are known for a lot,
such as mayhem, tribulations, havoc, and vexations.
The blighters never quit, keeping noses in a snit;
their attitudes icky-splicky, approaching them's tricky:
proceed with dread care or abandon your hair!

Should ya have no hopes left if they rob you bereft,
heed well their bellword, though completely absurd
and the meaning's obscure. Come closer to hear
as I whisper in huffs that they breathe in loud puffs.
Oh, I nearly forgot—you may need a graveplot
once The Withers are through. It is certainly true—

they bite worse than they bark and leave quite a mark.
All will need a Pallbearer, and Mortician of terror.
June Gloom a favorite color, naught could be duller.

Someplace out of eyesight they cluster at night,
ringing round a lamppost, singing sly as a ghost,
casting witherous stares, catching specters unawares
with their best imitations of immortal gyrations,
their gazes Jitterbugging as miffs lead to slugging
and you just never know how their temper will blow!
Powderkegs of Pepper, more shunned than a Leper
they lumber and stumble, lackadaisically mumble
and nibble rusty nails, flicking rabbit-proof tails.

Mincing morbid footfalls; squawking eerie birdcalls.
Categorically obtuse, they creep without excuse.
Thrice rude as Buffaloes stampeding over toes,
the wretches have no alibi for making kiddies cry.
Rancid shapes teeming walls, creaky rustles in halls,
at the gong of a clock scuttling back neath their rock.
Huddled chins to beak-noses, they strike the worst poses.
Ignore not a sound, for they might be around . . .
Batten well all the doors; guard any crack in floors.

Don't unlock to a knock or inside they will flock.
You can never get them out. Plug every single spout.
The Withers are coming, scrambling and humming!

Dream Lover

Michael Minassian

She carefully planted
flowers in her mouth,

well aware that at any moment
a tulip might spring

down the throat of her lover.

The Fall of the Damned

Jennifer Ruth Jackson

After the painting by Peter Paul Rubens

Archangel Michael kicks bodies into hell,
a cascade of the corpulent and corrupt.
A tangle of limbs flail—white flags for pale
skin—soon to be charred and marred
by fires and rocks below. Demons
(an afterthought of abyssal measure)
size up meaty rain, just out of view.
Those closest to the top could almost
climb the mortal staircase, but Michael's
boot rests like a cumulous cloud out of reach.

Rack's Last Run

Steven Withrow

I

Since Melcherville has only one old plow,
It doesn't take much snow to keep us in,
At least until the county clears the roads.
My neighbor, Mr. Rack, is out there now
Fighting the blizzard, trying to keep the loads
Of powder from amassing. He won't win,
Yet he told me once that plowing like he does,
Alone in his ancient pickup, makes him feel
Essential to the workings of the town:
"I might not be the strong young man I was
When two storms laid near sixty inches down
And cut the power a week, but I can deal
With whiteout nights as good as anyone."
Watching at a window, safe and warm,
As snowdrifts heap my garden beds outside,
I wonder if tonight is Rack's last run.
Some things just are; you don't get to decide
How long you stay out, driving, in a storm.

II

I sleep while Rack continues through the night.
In a dream I conjure up a wendigo—
Or, more precisely, a tall chimeric spirit
Emerging from the winter woods, all white

Except for amber fox's eyes. I hear it
Venting its breath in a slur of heavy snow.
More wind than flesh, it bellows hungrily.
My dreaming mind is channeling the threat,
Though I am not its target, I can tell.
I merely had the nerve to set it free
From prison in a fireless, frigid hell.
(I hope this is a dream that I'll forget.)
The wendigo has no mouth, but it eats
With its whole body, bestial in its way,
The phantom forms around it: ghosts of trees,
Smoky underbrush; even the tweets
Of what I see are birds—wrens, chickadees?
Consumption breaks; I wake; and it is day.

III
A county worker finds Rack's truck at dawn,
Abandoned in a culvert near the border
Of Melcherville and Ashe, ten miles due east
Of our quiet neighborhood. The TV's on;
A newsman speaks as solemn as a priest;
A helicopter shot shows rank disorder:
The pickup's on its side in a chasm of ice,
The rusted plow blade's broken off and bent,
And the driver's missing—Alden David Rack,

Age ninety. The photo shown is old but nice.
"The mystery is, not a single track
   Leads to or from the truck. The accident—
   Foul play is not suspected—has been referred
   To state authorities." I'm reeling still;
   It makes no sense. But something jogs my brain:
   An apparition of evil. "Foul" is the word.
   I *dreamed* the reason, though it seems insane.
   My wendigo grew famished enough to kill.

The Helrún's Hoard

Adam Bolivar

On a stone altar   a struggling hare
Lay in bindings   and lurched wildly,
His heart hastened,   heavy his breathing,
His eyes searching   for any escape.
The helrún held   a honed dagger,
Skillfully skinning   the screaming hare,
Whose blood coated   the baleful stone.
Moonstruck the mind   of the madwoman,
She scavenged the bones   from the scuttler's corpse,
Her hoard carried   in the hide of a fox,
Buried by starlight   in the black midnight,
A year later   yielding a harvest
Of pieces to join.   A puppet she wrought,
Strange string-led wight,   striding nimbly,
Spider's spellcraft,   speaking portents.

A Funerary Sound

Benjamin Blake

The mist rolled in
Thick and obfuscating.
Bestowing upon the village a deathly silence,
Only punctuated by the tolling of bells
Resounding through the empty streets.

Even the crows are tight-beaked,
And the only incandescent light
Emanates from a crossroads inn.
An unspoken invitation
Seeping through its windowpanes,
Whispering promises of womblike warmth.
Of the delicate sickening sin
That comes with broken time.

The lost souls
Inside those stone walls
Rarely speak.
And even when they stutter a muddled sentence
It comes from a year long past,
Back when they still truly breathed.

Poets of eternal despair
They recognise their kith and kin,

And offer an empty stool
On which to spend an aeon.

The crimson-painted door opens
And I cross the threshold
With shell-shocked hands.

Requiem

Yuliia Vereta

Teethless. Thumbless. Uneven. Vestigial.
But that's what we deserve to be in the end.
The day we managed to change the hearts
into the GMC engines we became the void.

The children we give birth to are born old.
With the time they grow younger, thinner,
and finally turn to ashes fitting the palm.
The world is not a subject to understand.

Nothing here is what it was, because now
everything is what it wasn't, rudimentary.
The life spins in an endless dance, singing
the requiem for what we once called *man*.

The Undying Folly

John Shirley

How much of vanity is unconscious self-defense
How much is simply pride? (putting up a fence)
How much of pomp is to hide behind the shine—
And fear is like a fire flickering 'neath a shrine

The priest of ancient gods, whether known or long forgot
Pretends belief in every fervent chant he taught
He drove his knife of flint into a sobbing child
Even as his own dark heart he secretly reviled

Egregores and nightmare-lords quiver in their mirth
They laugh at hopes arising with another birth
And now we pray as we gaze upon the creeping hearse
Unaware that arrogance has damned us with its curse

Psalms of the Lich Priests

Mark Howard Jones

Black blocks, mass piled upon lithic mass, to the very tip of its twisted towers, make up the cathedral that stands exalted and alone. From jagged pylons fly banners stitched from heretic pelts, bearing profane texts, flapping in the unceasing wind. Both sanctuary and prison, this place endures though all around it changes: one day desert, the next a forest of giant ferns, which gives way in turn to desolate marshland but a moment later.

Beyond the colossal carved stone doors, a dozen eyeless hierophants wait, each recalled from their death in the ash-pit tombs of cold Kethenar to pay a final penance. For a few drops of soul they will conduct you while the incense of corrupted flesh fills the air. Despite the aid of these cadaverous cicerones, it is wise to beware this treacherous space. Impossible architectures collide and collaborate to confuse the unprepared as precarious hollow spires and abyssal pits appear and disappear without warning. Remnants of the unwary and ill-prepared litter the cathedral precincts, forming an abstract pattern of failure and despair.

Darkness writhes on dried tongues as dead voices are raised in praise to nameless dark gods, the unspoken and unsung syllables echoing from the ornamented ogives. The black glass behind the massive main altar reflects uncertain shapes moving through the twilight filling the gargantuan space above the nave. Plaintive cries from extinct supplicants, trapped within that high space, interrupt the vocal devotions of the long-dead clerics as their voices begin to rise in praise, bidding to chant the past back into being. Truth and honesty, inconvenient and unwelcome, are reduced to ashes and served up in goblets of rue on feast days, when spiritual surgery is performed in the name of St. Nesiam of the Blade. A small nick or a cut to the quick, any deformities of the heart or mind are removed on days marked by the flying of a tattered black pennant. Formerly celebrants would kneel to drink like dogs at the decorative runnels set into the floor, filled with wine and blood flowing from the Chapel of the Bled Orphans, though now only desiccated hope provides succour.

Corpse honey drips from the towering altar like a madman's drool as the immortal children of profane passion pass by, forming a guard of honour for the shadowy sacerdotal figures as they advance, black filth flowing from beneath their rotting robes, emaciated hands raised in both balm and blame. It is rumoured that, when conditions are propitious, the double-skulled ecclesiast who leads them may divine the future by reading the blood stains patterning the floor in the claustrophobic *Cappela Dolor*, where wax accretions rise to the blackened ceiling from a half-millennium of burning votive corpse candles. Though the price for the service is one that most cannot pay.

*

From the boundary of the bleak horizon comes a wearied figure. Crouched and crippled, this envoy of the heresiarch advances towards the black cathedral, an inky nimbus of pain surrounding him. His hand, a red spider, clutches his cloak, adorned with letters taken from the names of the long dead, as he struggles toward the huge structure that stands, open but indecipherable, like an unreadable stone book before him. Though others before him have failed, he has spent a lifetime searching for this elusive architectural abomination.

Halting to lean against the tall marker stone, defaced with ancient unreadable graffiti, he removes a scroll from within his robes and begins to read. His words soak into the very air as water soaks into sand, gone within moments. In the void above, the stars glare down, shifting their aeons-held shapes, beginning to liquify and flow. The man watches as the star-cursed night descends, engulfing the spires and crawling across the buttresses to press against the lightless windows. Within, the stones vibrate and shift, sensing their fragility despite their gargantuan size. The night is a behemoth too powerful to resist and what has always stood must one day face ruin.

The night is an amorphous army, unstoppable and indestructible. The nocturnal starless cold marches on but, while devouring darkness flows in as the walls descend into nothingness, the cobwebbed congregants sit unperturbed. The disintegrating vaults echo with the sound of despairing devotion. Crumbling mouths caress the unforgotten words as the psalms of the lich priests fall silent, yielding to the orisons of dust and stillness.

"Blessed are the never born, for they know peace."
—spes perditus, The Penumbral Gospel

Behemoth

Steve Vertlieb

In dreams he walked along the edges of the beach
drawn each night to the brooding sea
his feet drank deeply of the warm, moist surface
infinite grains of sand sparkled in the moonlight
while lonely silence drenched his thoughts

Dying fish lay strewn along the water's edge
prone and vulnerable
struggling vainly to return to their watery womb
and birds swam silently above the clouds

The ground succumbed to the weight of his heart
and he fell, gasping for breath
the sea crushing his will
descending slowly to the ocean floor

Sensing the enormity of a shadow behind him
he turned in fear to find the ghostly shell of a once great ocean liner
a titanic monolith stretching endlessly
beyond his gaze toward the stars

He awakened, numb, a silent scream trapped in his throat
weakened by the disturbing frequency
of his nocturnal wanderings
yet instinct beyond time and imagining beckoned his return

Somnambulistic lethargy consumed his waking hours
the sun appeared somehow muted
the air stagnant and stale
a tangible layer of haze blanketed the city
the skyline a translucent mirage

Primordial longing urged him to return to the sea
yet the realization startled, and filled his soul with dread
he hovered tentatively above the street
a soulless marionette dancing fearfully
to a composition of unknown inspiration

Floating between waking and dreaming
he sensed the water's edge through peripheral consciousness
the sand baked beneath his feet
and he stumbled uncertainly toward the waiting shore

As he watched the darkening sunset
he felt a dreadful foreboding
birds cried above his head
and the earth screamed in terror

From somewhere far beyond the beach
he heard cataclysmic thunder
the eruption so deafening his ears could barely contain it

* * *

The clouds grew black, enveloping the dying horizon
the ocean rose from out of its cradle like a towering behemoth to meet
    the sky
he watched in wonder as the great wave approached
and eternal night engulfed his dreams.

Inheritance

Kendall Evans

Caterpillars fashioned
From festively colored graffiti
Beetles trimmed in tin
& toy mechanical crickets

Bend and release
Their metal blades
A snap-snap chirping sound—
While roaches scurry

On wire-thin aluminum legs
Their pyrite carapaces agleam
Like reflections in a golden eye
& scrawled graffitied forms

Come alive
Climb down walls
Cross the floor
While attaining three dimensions—

Eight-legged spiders
Of stainless steel
Weave webs
Capture struggling
Forms of squirming graffiti
Shroud their prey

In cocoons of silver strands—
A ladybug crowned with red

& black polka-dotted
Strides past regally
This queen of beetles—
Everywhere, all these creatures

Seething and inch-worming
Taking over the world
Artificially intelligent
Prolifically procreating

What chance
Do we humans have?
We have created
Our replacements

The Leaves

David Barker

In early fall we start to sense it near:
The coming winter days without respite,
A dreary span of time like endless night
When summer's easy joy's replaced by fear.
The wind-swept leaves dance light along the lanes
And spiral up to sky atop the hill.
Old poets sit by fires —they know the chill
Of hatred beamed to Earth from fungal brains.

On autumn eves the membrane grows most thin
That separates our world from outer space.
Our minds then link up to a distant race
Who thrive in far off Nithon's howling wind
That gusts across the gulfs between the globes
And thus, conveys to Earth their tendrilled probes.

Inspired by H. P. Lovecraft's *Fungi from Yuggoth* sonnet
"XIV. Star-Winds"

Ballet of the Marionettes

DJ Tyrer

A dozen figures upon the stage
Glide soundlessly into place
Each one hangs lifeless
Each a pallid mask for a face
Then they begin to dance
Performing their ballet peculiar
First the Homage to the King
Then the Sighting of the Dark Star
Their movements subtle
Their movements sublime
Yet strangely lifeless
Despite keeping time
Until at last the dance is done
They fall still with a sigh
Dangling marionettes
And the echo of a bitter cry

House of the Unholy

Jack Ranieri

He put on his best suit, as usual.
Then again, they are all the best.
He checked his hair and teeth.
Sheathing his work in their holsters.
Meditative preparation finished.

He embarks on his night's task,
Bound for a former house of God.
Our Lady of Peace is now a club,
The club a front for clandestinity.
With dark secrets buried below.

Outside he sees the laser lights,
Strobes glow through stained glass.
Atop the spire the crucifix is caged
Cellular arrays the cross's prison
A neon sign hangs over the façade:

"Hathor's Harem" emblazoned.
He arrives and engages there,
Breaching the desecrated threshold,
Alcoves once occupied by saints
Now hold shows of vice, of lust.

Hard bodies, soft skin dancing.
In the pulpit, a DJ preaches bass.
Beating music thumps the heart,
Ballet of lonely people grinding,
Finding comfort in shared sin.

He shadows through the throng
Like a stalking predator on a hunt,
Not looking for a meal but his mark.
A secret resides in the confessional,
Used for chemical comfort privacy.

After the junkies exit, he enters here.
Mirrored shelf with powder residue
Lifts to reveal a key pad card reader.
Enters a code, inserts stolen card,
The booth descends into the abyss.

Coming to rest in fluorescent labs,
His first obstacles fall so easily.
Silenced barrels. Rising smoke.
Club music masking screams,
Moving slowly and deliberately.

He's at a door with vault quality.
It's an unexpected level of security,
Trying to hack this door quite futilely.
Unexpectedly it parts before him,
Revealing opponents to folly him.

Brief moment of silence awkwardly,
Hand to hand is the combat now.
He blocks, he dodges, he strikes,
Repeating in various flavors here.
Now appears a bladed inconvenience.

The last guy, a big guy; charged fast,
Knife slashing with skill so brash.
Bullets spent, he must oblige him
With a spin here and a flourish there.
Now biggie is bleeding out, dying.

Into the armored room he enters,
Seeing all this exotic wonder here.
Beakers and technology impressing,
Above his pay grade these gadgets,
But the prize isn't hard to discern.

On a platform like a steel pedestal,
Encased in glass, are tubes ominous.
Is it liquid or is it light? Both maybe.
They glow with some divine source.
The bass from above still pounds.

He touches the glass, lights go out,
Plunged into the darkness uncertain.
Is this panic he feels? So foreign.
He grabs a tube of the illumination,
The glowing elixir is his torch now.

The clock is ticking and doors closing.
He rushes to catch the confessional,
But biggie's blood slicks his escape route.
He slides, he slips, the torch tube flies.
Clambering to catch it, he fails. It cracks.

He falls onto the luminous liquid freed,
With wounds open from his ingress.
He's quickly infected with this potion,
Pulse quickening and mind clouding.
Can confirm the mutation is devilish.

The killer now reborn a killer still
Clawing up the confessional's portal
Through the booth bursts a predator,
As if risen from Hell in stories of old.
Fear and debris dispersed generously.

The consummate professional gone,
What's come forth is simply profane.
The glowing fluid seeping from pores,
Swollen to preposterous proportions,
Severity unhinged and unspeakable.

They came into this church for release,
To commune in a perverted kind of prayer
Now the sanctuary's sinners went to ground,
A demon who transformed in the depths
Is preying on deconsecrated ground.

Historical References

Janice Klain

History, mystery, figures,
Dashed hopes wailing, new hopes calling out
Communications of betrayal, denials of acceptance, responsibility for
actions,
Yet a yearning, a pleading to be heard

bumps in the night, clunks in the day

Hoping, yearning, wanting to be heard—yet still wanting to hide.
We see you, we hear you, we're all here together;
Let's continue, not finish the conversation.
Do we help? are we helping? or do we leave you be?

clunks in the night, bumps in the day

Connecting through feelings, sounds, and static
Hear me, hear me!—we hear you, we see you, we feel your presence!
Fear not, we'll continue to carry on your story

Alas, Poor Love

P. S. Conway

a savage trinket from a love that's passed,
my Ophelia rests in her silent tomb.
a hand that once was warmed by mine, at last,
has found its way to my heart's secret room.

it came loose; what else was i meant to do?
a few quick tugs, and it was almost free.
just one clean slice through some stubborn sinew,
unfettered at last, it belongs to me.

i do not miss her touch, no, not at all,
for now it curls within my palm each night.
Alas, poor love!—i quiver at its pall,
a phantom trace of life before twilight.

she left me once, but now she understands:
true love's forever . . . give or take the hands.

Flinch

David C. Kopaska-Merkel

underdressed,
as if disinterred,
after more years
than I care to number,
shedding crumbles, and I,
shielding my new wife
from the sight of you,
blanched digit hovering
by the doorbell:
"Dad?"

The Venturers

Manuel Pérez-Campos

Hosted by unknown gods, the grotty darkness
of unsafe passage which buoys New York City,
that labyrinth of infinite delays where shouts
of caution are whispered under one's breath,
is anon materializing with the swift
strangeness of a mass hallucination throughout
Broadway—that built-in escapism
of behind-doors claustrophobic stages—an irregular
queue of bent-backed sauriany kaiju who exhale
gamma particles at will, each halfway as tall
as the first flag of a skyscraper and glimpsed
sporadically under mile-high acid rain only at
an obscuring angle as externalized
vertigoes with misdirection-proof gaze:
these avatars of insuppressible two-step
rumpus are truly the progeny of Thanatos:
and despite pill and/or smartphone anodyne,
they are strongly sensed under rivers of umbrellas
in the upper quadrant of one's background
by pedestrians attempting vigorously to cross
the no man's land between work site and cramped
apartment without leaving their chalked outlines
on the overburdened sidewalks as a result
of having been trampled on or otherwise
annihilated by one of these nameless hulking
phantom lurkers, their constant companions.

The Tomb of Nyarlathotep

Lauri Taneli Lassila

pyramids, incantations
abandoned necropoli
a dying chorus of horn
a death in gold—luxurious

the weight of the earth, of time
the silence of millennia, waiting
to happen, to enter our hearts
our canopy jars, our funerary labyrinths

endless lines of slaves, slaves
bled dry under the sun
vaporous, escaping
to gods waiting with their maws agape

sly we sleep, quiet
under the sun and the earth, hidden
sly we wait, silent
for the beginning of the end

for the opening of the doors
for the letting loose of the plague
for the extinguishing of the sun
for the loud cry of power

World's End Rhapsody

Ngo Binh Anh Khoa

The day begins like every other day
With people tending to their normal lives,
Not knowing what is fated to arrive
Till thunderous trumpets from the Heavens play.

Large pillars of light split the trembling skies,
From which a million wings of flame descend,
Whose countless eyes gaze down and swiftly send
The streets into cacophonous gasps and cries.

In orderly rows, the looming giants stay,
A most ethereal and majestic choir
Graced with the brilliance of celestial fire.
An otherworldly symphony starts to play.

The starting movement makes the oceans stir,
Wild whirlwinds thrash, and roused volcanoes roar
In concert, shaking the Earth to its core
And swallowing mortal screams throughout the world.

The second movement rises with the voices
Of Angels, making sunlight's radiance grow
Till all that mankind's built melt in its glow
While meteors dropped provide percussive noises.

Comes silence till the clear sounds of bells sweep
Across the remnants of the stainless sphere,
Heard by the purest of souls far and near
Till they are lulled into a peaceful sleep.

The final movement plays. The Angels hum;
The light of sun and moons and stars all fades.
Cocooned in black, the Milky Way's erased,
From dust created, now as dust become.

From out that void the Angels glide away,
Their task completed, their performance done.
Now let new weaves of cosmic dust be spun,
And from the dark shall come a brand-new day.

pilgrims, devotees, perversions and marionettes

Lee Clark Zumpe

are we nothing more than doting pilgrims,
affixed to hallowed shrines and tombs,
beguiled by silent charms, whispers,
and the strange witchery of autumnal shadows?

are we naïve attendees of the masquerade,
participants in Bacchanalian orgies,
devotees of decadence, desire, depravity
and the wicked designs of unseen divinities?

are we curious aberrations of nature,
perversions of evolutionary development,
fettered by a blighted genetic inheritance
orchestrated by apathetic alien architects?

or are we sad and hapless marionettes
dancing madly to discordant notes
played by unseen pipers at infernal revels
held in sepulchral chambers outside space and time?

The Oblivion Gut

Maxwell I. Gold

Past that gaping maw whose wide, dripping mandible swallowed that wretched sky behind craggy teeth, I saw the belly-bottom emptiness of oblivion, hot and infinite. Standing along a moist cliff-face, I gazed into the shaft below, black and barren, and traced a dark tunnel toward the hellish nether-scape whereupon every manner of ruined dream, crushed star-bone, and twisted atom-heap were compressed, prepared for digestion by that hungry, deep-beast.

And through those wild, crystalline spectral gas swamps, a putrescence, composed of gurgling doom-pockets and gravity extrusions, bends my brain with every relentless tick. Still, the beast, Entropy's bastard, wasn't quite content and reached beyond the event horizon, until the fabrics thought to compose reality were ripped as if they were nothing but pathetic tatters. My eyes bled with disillusioned faith, witnessing my own compromised reason: life and death merged into a sharp welcoming sensation when I saw the belly-bottom emptiness of oblivion, hot and infinite.

Noonday Demon

Scott J. Couturier

Ruddy corpse
Roaming abroad at noontide—
Nails like talons,
Fierce reddened eyes,
Body swollen with stolen blood—
This demon fears no sunlight,
But comes forth
To feed when summer's
Swelter is hottest—
Fangs & fetid breath,
Flies feasting in halo
On slaver of last gory repast—
Attacks occur indiscriminately,
Man or woman, child or beast—
Arteries torn avidly open
By bite of dagger-keen cuspids—
Suckling voracious until
Victims grow tallow-pale,
Then cast into fallow fields
To bloat & rot in July's heat—
Fiend of drought-dry furrow,
Unclean cadaver animacy lent
By some savage lust
To ravage & gorge to corpulence—
Coated with crimson curls

Of wiry, wolfish hair,
Vampire violating diurnal domain
With no resting place for lair—
He was a bad man, they say,
Before he fell & broke his neck—
Now a Noonday Demon,
Night's succor forsaken
To stalk for prey
On heath & highway—
Blasphemous barrow-monger,
Tearing out throats
With terrible teeth—
Clothed in clot-ridden rags
& plump to obscenity
With bounty of unseemly glut.

Lazarus

Wade German

And he returned to us estranged
    From wandering through death's still reach
    Whilst sepulchred for many days.
And all his aspect is deranged;
    And horrid depths are in his gaze
    That still surveys the deathrealm's reach:

His eyes! like voids of midnight jet
    That sear into our very souls
    With cold inhuman glares, that find
Old morsels of remorse, regret,
    To dredge up from our hearts and minds,
    The secret sewers of our souls.

Thus Bethany, in dread, has turned
    To exile him amongst the dead.
    He dwells that place he was entombed;
But to our horror have we learned
    Our ancestors have been exhumed—
    He speaks to desecrated dead . . .

But none of us will dare go near
    The ancient graveyard where he walks;
    For where he fits in which god's plan
Is now our all-consuming fear—
    Is he a resurrected man
    Or demon which amongst us walks . . . ?

At the Hairdresser's

Simon MacCulloch

Under the dryers the heads have deflated,
Prune-shrivelled skin-bags in phallic space helmets,
Drooped above glossy advertisement pages.
Don't look too closely, it isn't polite.
How can they talk with their jaws slopping over?
Maybe the helmets communicate, humming
Melodies stolen from Listen with Mother,
Stories that make the wigs stand up in fright.

Barbers will peck you with scissors and clippers,
Scything the fluff from your fidgety football;
Here at the hairdresser's everything's effortless,
Colours as lush as the tropical air,
Perfumes as slick as a chloroform kidnap,
Picking its victims from *Woman's Own* readers,
Never permitting a hint of a ransom;
Peer through the window and ask if you dare.

Under the dryers the dreams are luxuriant,
Budding and twining in deep pink miasma,
Spores drifting thick through the brain-spongy thought-clouds,
Foamed like a quivering blancmange on the seat.
That's when the hairdressers know it is finished;
Turn away quickly, you don't want to see them,
Stick-insect mandibles busy as scissors,
Swarming, descending and starting to eat.

Night Thoughts

Lori R. Lopez

My thoughts abound in the ink of a night
that no writer may wrestle onto a bare page;
the depths of a stillness profound as isolation,
that sound cannot penetrate or language translate
beyond this evisceral quietude's embrace . . .

Afloat upon vapors of intergalactic contrails,
at the speed of inspiration, terrors or anguish—
reaching, my fingertips almost touching a wisp
of words rotting, fragments forgotten or quite lost,
due to frailties of the intellect's starry dance . . .

Not scribbled in time, not lashed or weighted
with stones of metaphors and lucid replays.
Nor anchors cast to prevent hapless drifts
on giddy outward tides that could never return,
to be found by another like gold or flotsam . . .

Uncommonly releasing random scratches
tossed away without care, even a figurative bottle
to abide and soar, bob and ride the wild seas
into elsewheres I have rarely myself imagined,
all on a whimful supposition contorted . . .

How unlike me at all to show little restraint,
unleash like a demon these fanciful glib notions

of the soul and mind from a trunk in a rusted belfry
that may or may not be crammed with bodies
of tourists and neighbors who couldn't stay home.

I am not accustomed to letting go a single line,
which might even rhyme in this verse or that nursery;
possibly on a sheet stained with ballad or prose—
collecting reflectings my gibbous preoccupation,
bleeding darkly into jars from a cabinet of woes!

Horses and Homely Angels

Jessica Amanda Salmonson

There is a place called Grimy Heaven
Where the angels are all homely
And it rains a lot.
Shayne McGowan is there
And Lady Day
Groucho Marx as well; oh, and
Madalyn Murray O'Hair—
She's always so annoyed
And no one likes her particularly,
But she's there.

I'm the gal who nearly
Found for the world
The elixir of immortality.
In my laboratory I was so close
Way back in 1974
A week or two more
And I would have had it.

But then I got the news
That Jack Benny died
Which is when I said,
"Too late. What's the use?"
And burned all evidence
Of the formula.

I know I'm not
Suited to Paradise
But not nearly bad enough
For infernal realms.

I expect I'll be in Grimy Heaven
Where there are moonbows
In the rain;
The muddy streets are rank
Where dogs and horses shit.
It's sufficient for my needs
As I've only ever loved dogs
And horses,
And homely angels.

In Glastonbury's Walls

Adam Bolivar

In Glastonbury's walls   gladness abounded,
For Arthur was king,   his earls many,
And Géac was one,   youthful and waggish,
Cornish his mother,   kin to Saxons,
Heathens and Christians   halving his bloodlines.
Myrddin marvelled   at his matchless art,
The older man   envying the younger,
And at chess challenged   the cheerful rogue.
Stalemate it stopped: a strange ending.
A second game had   the same result,
Whilst the third threaded   a thorny path:
By magical means   Myrddin won it,
But bargained his soul   to bondage in Hell,
A bleak burden   for besting Géac,
Who tipped his king   with a toothy grin,
And wondered aloud   who won truly.

Heat Death

Jennifer Ruth Jackson

Darkness
sears flesh.
Come to bed
but first, turn
out the lights.
Let me smell
you in the sizzle
of smoke-coated
phantoms
while we scream
in unison.
Let us die
before we see
what feeds
on the hot
supper-steam
of us.

... and the Misfortune That Befell Her

Benjamin Blake

The gnarled branches dance
Outside the infirmary window
In the singular haunted half-light.

The Bible on the bedside table
Offers little relief,
From sins so obstinately succulent
As hers.

Fire cleanses all
But even the inferno was not enough,
Despite their best efforts.
One touch
Was all it took
For something in the shadows
To make a home
Within her withered heart.

And there it shall stay
Until the burnt shell of her corporeal frame
Shudders its last,
And it is released
Back into the crepuscular ether,
To patiently await
Its next unwittingly exquisite host.

The Morning After

LindaAnn LoSchiavo

"The Kill of the Wolf is the meat of the Wolf. He may do what he will."
—Rudyard Kipling, "The Law of the Jungle,"
The Second Jungle Book (1895)

The morning after, he's aware of red,
Five knuckles glazed with dried blood—probably
That fellow jogging. *Bald. Imagine that.*

Exhaling, savagery is shorn of fuss.

His heart no longer throbbing, extra teeth
Absorbed by his accommodating jaw,
Damp chest hair curling normally
In sweaty alphabets, he stands upright,
Embalming the night's pleasures, shame withheld—
As all shape-shifters must react. Regrets
Rest with the moon, whose puppet he's become.

I Am Glad That Graveyards Are Silent

Darrell Schweitzer

I am glad that graveyards are silent.
If the dead could speak,
What a monotonous babble they would make,
their stories so familiar, so trite:
I'm tired, let me rest,
I think I left something unfinished,
but I can't remember what.
All those vague, moaning sorrows,
lost loves, and old dreams
almost entirely faded even before
the dreamer stops dreaming.
I walk past the markers quickly.
I might stop and listen if I found
the grave of a murderer,
eager relish his secret crimes,
or, better still, a sorcerer where he waits
clutching a hideous talisman
until some greedy fool rips open his coffin
and unwittingly completes his transition
from death into ravenous, howling undeath.
At least the conversation would be interesting.
But no, the only howling I hear is the wind,
and the only voices I hear are the stones themselves

reminding me, without words,
as I close the gate behind me,
not to be so smug, because I
will be joining the rest soon enough.

As Long as We Remember

Geoffrey Reiter

"You'll live on in our memories." Well said!
So will your will then cradle my bright being
And swaddle my soul's sacred self and seeing
Beyond the earthly bourns in which I'm bred?
Can all the *me* my life means as I tread
This life alive be caught by you when fleeing
My frail form, sapient, wide awake, agreeing
That you may keep me conscious when I'm dead?

No? Peer into the clouded nebulae
That flame and flicker in the chill expanse,
And preach no more of memory and peace.
If memory is how I live, you lie
As I shall lie—life is no cosmic dance
But silence when the music-spheres must cease.

Amour Mort Immortel

Oliver Smith

An age has passed since I let fall your hand in this strange garden.
Long-abandoned, you and I; in love among the flowers
for years, sparkling in the radiant decay of blighted stars
reposed among briar-wound fawns, crumbled, fallen tritons
stone nymphs; age-rotted, immersed in green mosquito-pools

where perfumed air stifles life and growth; sepia-dappled blooms
lie submerged in the creeping toadstool's massed opalescence.
Inkcaps' deliquescent flesh stains tangled grass and moss
and alien lichens luminesce, stippled with putrefaction,
on the dusty, dried-out skeletons of foxgloves and poppy pods.

The garden's flamboyant heat draws diamonds from my skin
and my unsteady hand seems blotched with the plant's chlorosis.
I might have dead-headed the roses you left, tightly crumpled
and entombed, within their bud. I allow them to remain
in half-dreams of life; humidly resplendent with infection;

among the crooked stems and brown leaves, miasmas drift;
dim spectres conjured by the song upon my lips; a thing
bright, glistening in the night as if in a fever's sweat
again, again I sing of the dying earth's corruption
my desire stilled in the sweet music of oblivion.

The Welder

Ian Futter

The welder's arc of stinging sun
fuses flesh for an age to come,
in a misguided moment of weakness and need,
to the cold, dead dullness of the cyborg creed.

Hot spurts of metal spit and splutter.
Charred flesh, redundant, fills the gutter,
as the welder, pitiless, applies his trade,
reforming the structures nature made.

Bones are bonded to the metal bracing,
forests flattened by the concrete, racing,
as the welder's progeny augment his craft,
spewing his guile into every graft.

Chaos, bursting from creation's flaw,
risks expulsion, as the straight line lore
spurns spontaneity's libertine seeds,
and manmade flowers murder natural weeds.

Boundless form: immense design,
the structure stands inert in time,
and stretching upward, dust to star,
the frame distorts the stuff we are.

Now the welder's work is almost done,
his torch put out and the darkness come,
and each new babe, sprung from warm, wet womb
is deftly dropped into the welder's tomb.

The Tatters of Dead Gods

Maxwell I. Gold

In the broken bitter twilight where shadow-dirges moaned below spectral ruins of bronze temples and cerulean towers, I felt the heavy weight of Tomorrow press upon my embattled soul. These haunting reminders, warnings of what-was-to-come ripped apart my tired consciousness with anxious fervor. All around me, tattered and shredded emblems once worshipped by a people long forgotten lay wasted at my feet like the bodies of dead gods that no one cared to remember.

Faces, teeth, and bones soon broke through the nameless streets in a nameless city whose violent music clamored in my skull like it was trying to break free persistently musing, *no one remembers me.*

Gnashing and grotesque noises bellowed from behind my eyes, followed by blood and tears as if I felt the dirt and steel rip from under me in some horrible transformation. Piece by piece, the world crumbled in remnant shreds of both flesh and old shadow-dirges whose melodies haunted the voids betwixt darkness and death, until I found myself crushed beneath the weight of Tomorrow.

The Deathglow at Harrow Farm

Joshua Green

When night had fallen on the farm, it brought
A golden blight stillborn from sun and dust.
This glow came for an elding farmer fraught
With fear of deathly lights, of stars and rust.

He stood and peered beyond the dirty pane,
Upon tilled lands that teemed with silent life.
The orb flew 'tween the stalks to wither, drain
Until it met the man, a sharpened knife.

He held his seizing heart, then t'ward the glow
Expressed a heaviness so full of dark:

"Unravel me," he said. "Before we go?"

The sphere unwound to show a hillside marked,
A tomb where love had all but come undone,
Where slept the brittle bones of his young son.

The Thirst of Her Heart Is Not Fed

Oliver Smith

When your heart desires more than life, grown tired, and land abhors
your tread upon its shore, leave you the lonely starry skies
and barren broken life; come out among the reefs at night,
where beneath the summer moon, the sea's dead immortals rise.

Come sing, come play, come swim, come dive you among the urchins.
Your weary bones, enfold, in lascivious, purple flesh.
Come taste the kraken's lips; the wild embrace of starfish arms,
the crinoids tender touch, and anemones' viscous kiss.

For beneath life's vernier, in the deeper kingdom dwells
the naked sea. Unveiled; stranger things than the land can know.
Sea may make sweet again fouler things than the air can bring;
sea may make live again sweeter things than the wind can blow.

In memory unbound, from worlds lost before land was born,
this human mask grows thin, where swimmers bask in sea-green dreams,
this human mask grows thin, down among the brown kelp weed,
this human mask grows thin, as we shoal in the tidal stream.

In the deep abyss, in ocean currents, angels glide
and adore their idol in sea-carved caves and corals grown
far away from daylight. Beyond the cold misshapen shore,
they hold their gorgeous court in palaces of living stone

So far beyond the light, beyond the reach of bathysphere;
beyond the human heart, in ocean trench, from out the dark
and to the dark returned, with ancient long-remembered gods,
and in the darkness deep, we dwell and wait, as eons pass.

Upon the land, in creeping time's disguise awhile, we bide
the end of humankind; when the hammer of stormy tides
with eldritch wave and wind casts down the cliffs and drowns the town
grinds cities into sand and swallows down the mountains high.

Hyde

Lee Clark Zumpe

I hear it stirring in its cage—
    a treacherous, sleek beast
    with arched back and open mouth,
flashing eyes that blaze with indignation.

I hear it growling and snarling—
    a grim, savage creature
    ruled by primal passions,
voicing its violent intentions.

I hear it gibbering in the dark, alone—
    a murderous mixture of feigned timidity
    and antagonistic boldness,
keen to strike a Faustian bargain.

I hear it mocking me from the shadows—
    a cunning, perceptive predator
    toying with its prey
before turning toward its monstrous nature.

The Black Shepherd

Adam Bolivar

The Black Shepherd   bides in shadows,
Shimmering his lantern,   shining wanly,
To make mischief   on a moonless night.
Wayward rovers,   bewitched by the spark,
Follow it further   into the fearful heath,
Ghostlight guided.   Godly his power,
The Shepherd makes   a sharp judgment,
Granting the guileless   a grim ending,
Drowned, death-taken   in deep water.
The worthy he picks   for his wonton flock,
Leading them safely   with his light's flicker,

A spark kindled   in the spry-witted,
Heart heathen-turned   who heeds its call.

Chance Meeting

Jennifer Ruth Jackson

It begins with a shortcut home
through a long alley like a throat
open for a sword. It continues
with shadows & shuffled footsteps . . .

not yours. It goes on. You swore
you should've a hit street miles ago.
It ends with the rats, your scream,
& the not-quite-human in the dark.

Lost Love

DJ Tyrer

Yearning for what cannot be retained
Unable to abandon desire, pass on
Remaining trapped in between
One foot in both worlds
Those of the living and of the dead
Seeking the warmth of mortal love
To give breath once more to dead flesh
But, finding only terror and screams
The condemnation of the grave
Trapped, tormented, terrible of form
Yearning turns to bitterness
Love to ashes and to hate
Becomes a horror to its victims
And, ultimately, to itself

Butterfly-Boy

Dmitri Akers

Beyond the screens of dreams, I pen this now:
A tale of fancy, known to minds obscene . . .
I woke one day to sweating, shakes, and gasps,
As window-shutters broke and Death himself
Began to rasp as loud as hornet-nests,
Within the rimy night, I woke and turned
And, tugging sweaty sheets to thumping heart,
I nearly screamed to see these visions come,
From out the deepest circle Hell may keep!
Above my bed there floated wisps of dread,
A swirling host of phantoms, wraiths, and ghosts,
Of every hue of white and every green.
Amongst their numbered dead I saw
His pallid face with sunken eyes and tears
Of black that streamed along his scars,
This ghastly face, a murdered boy of nine,
Began to twist and bend into a fae's,
With insect eyes and sucking proboscis,
A boy transformed into a butterfly!
It sloughed a chrysalis of flesh and skin
That dropped upon my bed with bloody splats;
Careening o'er my bed with shrillest squeals
This ghost emitted sonic sounds of dread
And flapped those toxic wings with impish might
Until it spun its webby silk above my head,

A horrid screen of deathly whites so pale,
It spun that sticky, magick thread of silk,
Until I became its thrall that merely crawls
Inside the walls of silk, this dream-cocoon.
I sleep inside this womb of samite sheets
And suck upon the teat that spits its warmish milk . . .
I never wake from dreams of butterflies;
Instead, I live inside this horrible web of plies,
To realise that men may never sleep
As long as dreams may haunt the minds of men.

Incident in the Cells of Dream

Scott J. Couturier

An incident in the cells of Dream:
Where I thought a close captive alike to me,
So readily did we gabble through those
Walls of gemstone honed to opacity
Which make up the mass of that dungeon.
We spoke of much that made us assume
The other was similar, especially our pining
For familiar trees & grass, & our love of starlight.
We knew selfsame names for constellations—
Many incidences in our discourse
(Beyond us sharing a kindred tongue,
Though one speaks all tongues in Dream)
Disposed us to supposing the other
From some similar world, perhaps even
That very same weary iteration of Earth.

After long weeks of frustrated effort,
I managed to chip away a bit of the elfin
Mortar binding a low-set stone in place.
Pulling it aside, I peered into the darkness
Of my fellow captive's cell & called:
"Here I am! Finally I loosened & drew aside
A stone; come close, so I may see you!"
For a beam of mealy light shone through the
Bars marring my cell door, casting
A sickly & malingering illumination.

*   *   *

In that obscured beyond I heard a scuffle,
Then an indrawn breath, as of alarm.
Slowly They crept closer to me, & I bent down
My head to the floor, the better to see.
Emerging into that dim ray appeared
A countenance of unspeakable nightmare,
Profoundly unsettled & disordered,
Wriggling as if wrought of fell jelly,
& awrithe with tentacles tipped by iridescent eyes!
These weird planes of physiognomy defied
Easy processing by my untethered senses.

Our screams mingled with many in that prison.
Simultaneous to my shocked horror & dismay,
This mate in captivity shuddered away
From my own aspect, to Them equally accursed
& onerous to sanity's utmost brink.
Mutually we wailed, in lunacy's grip:
With manic thrust I re-blocked the chink.

Kin not of flesh, but of what we think!
Now, mutually mad, we converse as before
Through barrier of cruelty-blackened stone,
Raving through this newfound night of fright
Till They decay to mutant froth & I to bone.

The Brood of the Jaguar Goddess

Manuel Pérez-Campos

Gauntly upright in sapphire-encrusted headdress
and in a loose robe of silk as white as a cataract upon a throne of peridot
chiseled to appear the confluence of sun and moon encoiled
by an anaconda, her gaze as devious as a philosopher's thought,
the one who can insert with a turn of her wrist
the carrion-elated cry of the condor in the breast
of an agitator blanches deeply, overcome by a sublime tremor
as the priest intermediaries in their feathered regalia,
learned in calendrical astronomy, gathered there to appease
with their own lives if necessary the lust
which has already decimated half the kingdom kneel
and turn their strained faces between outstretched hands
to the vast ancient dampness of the stonework floor.

Matter at its most extreme transcends
the limits of reason, and she—arrived
in their immemorial past from
agoraphobic-eliciting regions of unawakened starlight,
in the form of an aerolite encased in
a red flame shaped like a teardrop
is made of such matter.

The one who can maintain her regal stress posture
indefinitely elongates into an arcing shadow

from which robe and headdress fall and hits the tract
before them as a crouching sleekness made of black light
and which their caste for innumerous generations
have called a jaguar, because there is nothing
that is closest in their experience to its shape.

Her psychokinetic gaze dissolves all at once them who
to honor her call themselves her brood
into a long draft of rippled air quasi-animated
by confused whispers and half screams and which she sucks in
through jaws agape to sustain the intra-atomic balance
which keeps her extant in this far-off world,
an interminable void away from the one she dimly recalls.

After a series of impatient low growls,
when the digestion of their essences
is complete, it reverts to that human manifestation
they have come to venerate:
and as she rises with slow deliberation and re-occupies
with naked hauteur the throne, alone in the cyclopean underground
palace they have carved in deference to the one
they call their dreamcatcher, having taught them to build the step pyramids
and whose aura of utter alienness inspires such dread
none can accompany her for more than a few pale blind
centipedes gliding across her indifferent hibernating

cheekbone before succumbing to madness, anguished
beyond endurance at having confirmed
telepathically yet again with despairing audacity for the nth time

that she is indeed the last of her especial kind, resolves to amble
that very evening under the weariness of a gibbous moon
terminally into the repercussive breakers out of a gravelled path
lined with anachronistic cycads in full knowledge
that the unheard-of event that is their barbaric civilization,
that interlocking officious mass of superstitious rites
executed with climatic heart-extracting zealotry,
cannot exist in its present form unless
around the central unsolvable mystery that is she.

Dust to Dust

Ngo Binh Anh Khoa

I. The Dream

I wake up from another dream
In which our universe burned
Inside a boundless yawning maw,
All things to dust returned.

With sweat-soaked flesh, I clutch my chest,
Each gasping breath a toil;
The pain of being ripped to shreds
Still makes my insides roil.

My body trembles, for I know
What I saw is no dream
But a grim vision of our fate;
I thus choke on a scream.

II. The Memories

I've had these haunting visions since
My troubled childhood days,
When my own father, mad with grief,
Fell viciously from grace.

The loss of his beloved wife
Made his heart bitter, cold

As he sought solace in dark arts
And blasphemous crafts untold.

I watched as he searched far and wide
For old grimoires and texts,
And I was but a helpless child,
Afraid of what came next.

I still recall the stormy nights
When he'd recite strange spells,
And when no miracle came about,
I'd face my personal Hell.

My skin still bears the welts and scars
Born of his sweltering rage.
Chained down by filial piety, I
Remained trapped in his cage.

The torturous days stretched into months,
And soon a year went by;
Plagued by his bouts of lunacy,
More traumatized was I.

And then a breakthrough he would find
Within a flesh-bound tome,
Which he abused his post to gain
And have that thing brought home.

Some alien tongue possessed his lips
As he read from that book,
And all the while his face assumed
A terrible, manic look.

From where I hid, I saw him prowl
Around his cluttered space
To find things to draw hastily;
A circle filled the place.

More incantations passed his lips
Before they turned to screams
That echoed in the shivering air—
How they still haunt my dreams.

His heart's desire was granted then,
A miracle and a curse,
Which spread on his disfigured face
And festered, ever worse

Till his face was not his alone,
Nor was his scratchy voice.
His office and his private room
Were filled with anguished noise.

Each time I saw his bandaged head,
His foetid odor grew,
That of a decomposing corpse
Possessed him, through and through.

But from then on he'd hide away
And torment me no more;
I had become a squatting ghost
Inside his house, ignored.

I waited as time flew by till
I was, at last, of age,
When I fled from that place for good,
My future a blank page.

Or so I thought I had escaped
The shackles of my past.
Some hidden chains, though, still remain
And through the decade last.

III. The Visions

The night my father cast his spell
To summon what he sought,
My eyes went temporarily blind
When some stray dust they caught.

Since then I've always seen strange sights
When my eyes close in sleep:
A seaside kingdom with three moons,
Whose corpse-pale waters weep;

A city underneath the waves
Where something, slumbering, lies
Across strange aeons in which Death
In time eventually dies;

An otherworldly landscape where
Large tentacled shadows loom,
Or where some winged and faceless beasts
Drop men unto their doom;

A desert of our primal world
Ruled by a pitch-black man
Whose thousand faces, thousand forms
Sow madness through the land;

A cold plateau that shifts across
Innumerable planes,
And glimpses at some farms that store
Jars of still-living brains.

And more unearthly sights I'd see
In nameless realms afar,
Among which is an eldritch court
Illumined by the stars.

And this is what I'd dream of most
When sleep takes me at night,
Each session longer than the last
Until the final sight.

I'd dream of loud, monotonous flutes
That fill the boundless space,
Played by a large, inhuman shape
With shadow for a face.

I'd dream of planets circling nigh,
Each one a shrieking sphere,
Whose cries attract wild bat-winged things
That madly dance and jeer.

I'd dream of violent winds that howl
And flames that seem alive,
Which, ever raging, crackle and
Beneath the starlight thrive.

And at the heart of that dark realm,
A tumorous entity sleeps,
Its numerous eyes sealed by the flutes
Whose sounds eternally bleed.

The God to whom those beings bow
In worship and in fear
Rules all that was, is, and will be,
No other may come near.

My dreambound voyages take me
Through that chaotic world;
Each time, the veil between that realm
And our own further blurs.

Until the dreams begin to show
The cancerous thing awake,
And all the Universes are
Then torn apart and break.

Each opened eye has one more world
Into oblivion thrust.
Each yawning maw makes one more realm
Reduced to cosmic dust.

And I relive the agony
Again, again, again!
I cannot fathom how I've not
Gone utterly insane.

Perhaps the blast of mystic dust
Caused by my father's spell
Helped me retain a functional mind
Within this cyclic Hell.

But I would spiral when aroused
So brutally from sleep;
I'd hear a voice ring in my ears,
Choked up as it would weep.

It'd take a while till I find out
It's my strained voice that cries,
Which echoes in a hollow room
And in the silence dies.

IV. The Anchor

I sit on my damp bed and try
To regulate my breath,
To claw my way out of the pit
Upon my latest death.

I will my eyes to look around
And name five things I see:
My nightstand, glasses, phone, and lamp,
And something black near me.

I will my hands to move about
And touch four things nearby:
My plushies, pillows, bedspread, and
Soft fur that makes me sigh.

I will my buzzing ears to take
In three things I can hear:
The leaking faucet, ticking clock,
And purring in my ear.

I will my stuffy nose to smell
Two scents I can make out:
The stench of scattered clothes and some
Sweet scents that waft about.

I will my leaden tongue to move
And taste the tang of blood
Before a foreign presence boops
My lips with a soft thud.

I blink against the haziness
Until my vision's clear;
A small smile forms on my lips at
A sight so near and dear.

My black cat's amber orbs stare straight
Into my widened eyes;
Her purring calms me down as she
Upon my shoulder lies.

Her silken fur caresses me
And helps me to calm down;
Her moist tongue tickles me and grounds
Me to the here and now.

A chuckle bubbles up and spills
Out of my mouth right then;
Which joins the purring. How I wish
This peace would never end.

I do not know how long we've sat
Together in the dark;
This quietude is unlike before,
The difference truly stark.

My heartbeat gradually returns
Back to its normal pace
As my tears are wiped by the tongue
Against my reddened face.

V. The Repose

Wrapped in the silence, I can feel
Time idly ticking by,
And when my gaze turns to the clock
I realize dawn is nigh.

I almost get up to prepare
To go to work, but then
My cat's snores echo in my ear;
I stay still in the end.

A lazy day would help stitch up
My sanity's fraying threads;
I send a message on my phone
And lie down on my bed.

I gently move the slumbering cat
Till she lies on my chest
And let my head forget the dread
In favor of some rest.

Though dwindling down, the fear remains,
Still simmering in my mind,
But if our world's demise is Fate,
Our doom is by Design.

There's no escape the ultimate end
When that dark thing's awake;
I'm but a man that by chance sees
The Truth of what's at stake.

And I'm just that: a mortal man—
A lonesome speck of dust
Against that cancerous cosmic mass;
My warnings few would trust.

And even if some trusted me,
What could we possibly do
To stop it or convince the world
That what we say is true?

I could sit still and count the days
To our impending doom,
Or I can learn to live with it
And let my life resume.

My gaze once more falls on my cat—
A stray once, now my queen.
If I just laze around to death,
Who will tend to this fiend?

This loaf of fluff depends on me,
And I depend on her—
My anchor to reality.
I smile and stroke her fur.

So come what may, I'll strive to live
As long as I draw breaths,
Beside this cat, my dearest friend,
Until our destined deaths.

There's still some time before she wakes
And our day will begin.
We'll have some food and broken plates;
For now, though, we'll sleep in.

I welcome her sweet lullaby
And let it burrow deep;
The gentle rumbling lowers me
Into a dreamless sleep.

Classic Reprints

The Lorelei

Heinrich Heine

A sense of sadness troubles me,
And yet I know not why;
A legend ever haunts my thoughts
A tale from days gone by.

The air is cool, the skies are dim,
The Rhine pursues its way;
The mountaintop is glistening
In the dying light of day.

A maiden fair to look upon
Is sitting calmly there;
Her golden jewels glint and gleam,
She combs her golden hair.

She combs it with a golden comb
And sings a song the while,
A song of wondrous melody,
Intended to beguile.

The sailor in his little sloop
Is dazzled by her spell;
To her alone does he give heed,
As waves about him swell.

The sloop, I fear, is swallowed up,
The sailor too is caught;
And this is what the Lorelei
Has with her music wrought.

[Heinrich Heine's "Die Lorelei" was first published in 1824. Translated from the German by J. G. Maybrook.]

]

The Haunted Forest

J. H. Fowler

There is a forest, wild, vast, and dim;
  And a horror hangs in its vistas lone;
And Time, long toiling, an aspect grim
  Has over its mighty tree-trunks thrown.

And many path that far into it leads,
  To solitudes, sombre, solemn, and dread,
Is tangled with writhing and grisly weeds,
  All clammy and bloated, with rank dew fed.

'Tis a haunted forest: fantastic things
  In the gloom of its bird-shunned thickets lurk;
And its depths are thrilled with weird mutterings;
  And an influence strange is for e'er at work.

In the heart of that forest a Woman dwells,
  She is beautiful—oh! she is wondrous fair;
But for ever she weaveth unholy spells;
  And her eyes have a still and eerie stare.

Should a traveller bold near the precincts range
  Of that Woman's arbour, in shades remote,
He might hear in the stillness a harmony strange—
  A spell-song with a bewitching note.

And if to that siren strain he yield,
    And follow further the forest track.
Then woe unto him! for his doom is sealed:
    That hapless traveller will ne'er come back;

And who is that Woman of beauty wild?
    What fearful secret with her doth dwell?
Is she that queen of weird beings—the child
    Of some fallen angel? Ah! who can tell!

Oh! a fear-fraught realm is that forest old,
    With its trees primeval, and cankered core;
And Desolation her court doth hold,
    Deathlike, on its margin evermore.

[First published in *Outward Bound* (January 1915): 3. Thanks to Josh Callahan for providing the text of this poem.]

Reviews

Verse and Prose from New York

S. T. Joshi

LINDAANN LOSCHIAVO. *Always Haunted: Hallowe'en Poems.* n.p.: Wild Ink Publishing, 2024. 74 pp. $12.99 tpb.
M. G. TURNER. *Dreams of the Romantics: A Story Cycle.* New York: Riverside Press, 2025. 84 pp. $18.00 tpb.

Having just published her eighth book, LindaAnn LoSchiavo has quietly emerged as a leading figure in contemporary weird poetry. The current volume—printed in an oversize 7 × 10 format, perhaps the better to present Erin Caldwell's enticing full-page illustrations—can only add to her reputation.

There is no doubt that LoSchiavo—as with so many other poets, weird or otherwise, over the last several centuries—is inspired by prior literature in her own poetic work. "Secrets of the Spell" in part evokes Shakespeare's *Macbeth*, specifically the witches who make a baleful appearance at key moments in the play: "Mark my words: women have always fought back, / Preserved infernal mysteries. Bewitched. / Dark invocations learned by stealth live on." Washington Irving is summoned in "A Sleepy Hollow Hallowe'en"; Bram Stoker's Dracula makes an appearance in several poems. Most piquantly, in "Elizabeth Siddal Rossetti, Cemetery Superstar" (a poem first published in *Spectral Realms*), we read of how Dante Gabriel Rossetti buried many of his unpublished poems with the corpse of his wife, but later dug them up. As LoSchiavo pungently remarks, "Rossetti's poems sweetened maggots' meals."

But LoSchiavo also finds inspiration in music: Mussorgsky's most famous composition is the source of the poem "Night on Bald Mountain." Even more interestingly, strange incidents from real life, both old and new, serve as the bases for some of the most evocative poems in the book. We are taken back to the late eighteenth century in an "abecedarian" (a twenty-six-line poem in which each line begins sequentially with a different letter of the alphabet), "Honeymoon Homicide, Spring Street, 1799," recounting a still unsolved murder of a woman in Manhattan. By contrast, "Hallowe'en Horror, October 31, 2005," speaks ominously of the depredations of a journalist, Peter Braunstein, still serving his sentence in a New York penitentiary.

LoSchiavo varies her poems in verse with prose poems of exquisite delicacy and power, such as "Our Lady of the Holy Death," dealing with a shop dealing with death: "I pay tribute, my fists filled with miniature icons, melted wax, molten magma, the moan of a mystical *derecho*, a sword lily, and a clutch of shiny, obsidian feathers." "Poltergeists on President Street" is a vivid portrayal of those mysterious entities, referred to "vaudevillians of the void, greedy for a live audience." "An Ideal Lost in Night-Mists" begins as a poem in verse but shifts gears to prose, where an American coed flirts via text message with Dracula—then disappears.

Always Haunted will undoubtedly add its substantial weight to LindaAnn LoSchiavo's reputation as a preeminent weird poet, and one who has a particular gift of transmogrifying both the historical and contemporary elements of her native New York into verse that is chillingly memorable.

M. G. Turner is also a New Yorker. His *Dreams of the Romantics* is a series of prose fictions, but as it deals with several of the leading poets of the Romantic period, there is ample justification for reviewing it in these pages. The occasion for this story cycle is the most famous literary contest in the history of weird fiction—the gathering at the Villa Diodati (in the town of Coligny, near Lake Geneva, Switzerland) in 1816 when Percy Bysshe Shelley, Mary Shelley, Lord Byron, and John William Polidori sought to write the most effective weird tale. Percy and Byron wrote nothing or next to nothing; Polidori produced the able short story "The Vampyre"; and Mary wrote *Frankenstein*.

Turner envisions Mary being inspired to write the tale by hearing another great poet, Samuel Taylor Coleridge, recite *The Rime of the Ancient Mariner* at her home of her father, the philosopher William Godwin. Later, Coleridge reads his other great weird poem, *Christabel,* to an appreciative audience. In the story "One Night in Geneva," Turner engages in the fantasy of being himself a member of the literary circle at the Villa Diodati, recounting his own Gothic tale. Then, in "The Last Journal of the Good Doctor John Polidori," he imagines a lengthy diary entry by Polidori, written on 24 August 1821, featuring an account of his troubled relations with "My Lord" (i.e., Byron), who admitted to the physician a taste for human blood. Byron gives Polidori five years to cure his ailment; after much toil, Polidori finds the remedy—but then refuses to let Byron have it: "This would remove My Lord's bloodlust, and though this was what we had been hoping for, it would remove his immortality too." The diary entry was written on the date of Polidori's death. The final story in the book, "The Last Voyage," is a gripping modern recreation of the fateful boat trip that led to Shelley's drowning in the Bay of Spezia in 1822.

Dreams of the Romantics is a vivid and engrossing little book, although it could have benefited from a little more care in the use of archaic diction and in copyediting overall (e.g., the volume that contained the *Ancient Mariner* is *Lyrical* [not *Lyric*] *Ballads*; the verb "morphed" would probably not have been used in the early nineteenth century, which would have favored "metamorphosed" or some such locution). In spite of these small blemishes, it is well worth reading by those many devotees of the weird who find themselves drawn back to that day, more than two centuries ago, when several towering literary figures sought to enshrine the weird into the corpus of English literature.

Notes on Contributors

Dmitri Akers is a poet of the weird, living on Kaurna country. He writes in the weird poetic tradition, after George Sterling and Clark Ashton Smith. His poetry has appeared in *Spectral Realms, Midnight Echo,* and *Infernal Mysteries; or, A Compendium of Gothic Reveries & Dolorous Tales.* His short stories have been published in *Penumbra, The Skull & Laurel,* and *Spawn II: More Weird Horror Tales about Pregnancy, Birth, and Babies.*

Manuel Arenas is a writer of verse and prose in the Gothic Horror tradition. His work has appeared in various anthologies and journals including *Spectral Realms, Penumbra,* and *Weird Fiction Quarterly.* He has two collections of prose and poetry available at Jackanapes Press: *Book of Shadows* (2021) and *The Burning Ember Mission of Helldorado* (2024).

David Barker has been writing supernatural fiction and poetry since the 1980s. His latest book is *12 Foot Skeleton Poems.* David's work has appeared in many magazines and anthologies, including *Fungi, Cyäegha, Weird Fiction Review, The Audient Void, Nightmare's Realm, Forbidden Knowledge, Spectral Realms, The Art Mephitic, A Walk in a Darker Wood, A Walk in a City of Shadows, For the Outsider: Poems Inspired by H. P. Lovecraft,* and *Weird Fiction Quarterly.*

F. J. Bergmann edits poetry for *Mobius: The Journal of Social Change* and imagines tragedies on or near exoplanets. His work appears irregularly in *Analog, Asimov's, Polu Texni, Pulp Literature, Silver Blade,* and elsewhere. *A Catalogue of the Further Suns,* a collection of dystopian first-contact poems, won the 2017 Gold Line Press poetry chapbook contest and is available at fibitz.com.

Benjamin Blake is the author of the novel *The Devil's Children* and the poetry collections *Standing on the Threshold of Madness, Southpaw*

Nights (poetry and prose), *All the Feral Dogs of Los Angeles* (with Cole Bauer), *Dime Store Poetry*, and *Tenebrae in Aeternum* (published by Hippocampus Press). He lives in Abruzzo, Italy, and is currently at work on an autobiographical novel, *The Wolves of Montebello*.

Adam Bolivar, a native of Boston now residing in Portland, Oregon, published his weird fiction and poetry in the pages of *Nameless*, the *Lovecraft eZine*, *Spectral Realms*, and Chaosium's *Steampunk Cthulhu* and *Atomic Age Cthulhu* anthologies. Hippocampus Press published his collections *The Lay of Old Hex* in 2017 and *Ballads for the Witching Hour* in 2022.

William Clunie is an American poet living in Berlin. His work has appeared in *Dreams and Nightmares*, *Star*Line*, and as a collection from Demain Publishing, *Laws of Discord*. He would like to think his primary influences are Shakespeare, Milton, and Poe. He is married to a German woman named Sandra. They are quite happy together.

P. S. Conway is a two-time Pushcart Prize nominee with more than sixty published poems. He serves as the 2024–25 Poet-in-Residence for the Fictional Café. His debut poetry collection, *Echoes Lost in Stars*, was published in March 2024 to high critical acclaim. In April 2025, Conway released a satirical essay collection, *Life Sucks*. His writing oscillates between darkly literate and delightfully unhinged.

Scott J. Couturier is a Rhysling Award–nominated poet and prose writer of the weird, liminal, and darkly fantastic. His work has appeared in numerous venues, including *The Audient Void*, *Spectral Realms*, *Tales from the Magician's Skull*, *Space and Time Magazine*, *Cosmic Horror Monthly*, and *Weirdbook*; his collection of weird fiction, *The Box*, is available from Hybrid Sequence Media, while his collection of autumnal & folk horror verse, *I Awaken in October*, is available from Jackanapes Press.

Livia E. De Souza lives in Connecticut, where she writes fiction. Her short stories have appeared in publications including *Penumbra*, *Tales to*

Terrify, and *Amazing Stories*. She has written two novels: *The Blackdog King* and *The Sons of Saints*. Her novella, *The Case of Ruth Doyle*, will be released in the summer of 2025.

Kendall Evans's poems have appeared in *Asimov's*, *Dreams & Nightmares*, *Star*Line*, *Analog*, *Spectral Realms*, *Weird Tales*, and many other periodicals and anthologies. He is also the author of the novels *The Rings of Ganymede* and *Tales of the Chinese Pirate Princess Ching Shih*.

Ian Futter began writing stories and poems in his childhood, but only lately has started to share them. One of his poems appears in *The Darke Phantastique* (Cycatrix Press, 2014), and he continues to produce dark fiction for admirers of the surreal.

Adele Gardner's poetry collection *Halloween Hearts* is available from Jackanapes Press. With poems and stories in *Analog*, *Clarkesworld*, *Strange Horizons*, *Daily Science Fiction*, and more, Adele curated the 2019 SFPA Halloween Poetry Reading and serves as literary executor for father, mentor, and namesake Delbert R. Gardner.

Wade German's most recent full-length poetry collection is *Psalms and Sorceries* (Hippocampus Press, 2022). His first collection, *Dreams from a Black Nebula*, is also available from Hippocampus Press. Other titles include several slim volumes of his selected poems with Portuguese translation, most recently the chapbook *Noctivagations* (Raphus Press, 2024).

Maxwell I. Gold is a Jewish-American multiple award-nominated author who writes prose poetry and short stories in cosmic horror and weird fiction with half a decade of writing experience. He is a five-time Rhysling Award nominee and two-time Pushcart Award nominee.

Joshua Green is an author of weird fiction, fantasy, and science fiction. His work has appeared or is forthcoming in *British Fantasy Society: Horizons*, *Strange Aeon*, *Spectral Realms*, *Penumbra*, *Calliope Interactive*, and elsewhere. He has three wonderful children and a miniature Australian shepherd named Juni.

Jennifer Ruth Jackson is a poet and fictionist with cerebral palsy. Her work has appeared in *Strange Horizons, Vinyl Poetry and Prose, Algebra of Owls, Apex Magazine,* and elsewhere. Her poetry collection *Domestic Bodies* came out in 2023 from Querencia Press. When she isn't writing (or engaging in activism), you can find her crafting a variety of things or playing video games with her husband.

Mark Howard Jones lives and writes in Cardiff, the capital city of Wales. He has edited both volumes of *Cthulhu Cymraeg: Lovecraftian Tales From Wales.* His latest collections of weird fiction are *Star-Spawned: Lovecraftian Horrors* and *Strange Stories and Tales from the Rain: Early Weird Fiction* (both Macabre Ink).

With a background in the arts (non-dark), customer service and administration, travel, and tourism, and education, **Janice Klain** has plenty of experiences to draw from as she journeys through the world of the written word.

David C. Kopaska-Merkel won the 2006 Rhysling Award for best long poem (for a collaboration with Kendall Evans), and edits *Dreams & Nightmares* magazine. He has edited *Star*Line,* an issue of *Eye to the Telescope,* and several Rhysling anthologies. His poems have been published in *Analog, Asimov's, Strange Horizons,* and elsewhere. *Some Disassembly Required,* a collection of dark speculative poetry, won the 2023 Elgin Award. His latest collection, *Unwholesome Guests,* was published in 2024 by Weird House.

LindaAnn LoSchiavo is a native New Yorker, poet, writer, and dramatist. In 2024 she had three poetry books published in three different countries; two titles won multiple awards. In 2025 two titles are forthcoming: *Cancer Courts My Mother* and *Vampire Verses.* A segment of her formal verse functions as dispatches from the Bar-do—that liminal space she escapes to with her imaginative alter-egos and her Gothic predilections.

Lauri Taneli Lassila is a scribe of the unnamable from the border town of Tornio, Finland. Lassila's published literary works include poetry, aphorisms, essays, and speculative fiction. In English, his short story "The Root King" was included in the anthology *Azathoth: Ordo ab Chao*, edited by Aaron J. French and published by JournalStone.

Lori R. Lopez is a quirky author, illustrator, poet, and songwriter who likes to wear hats. Her Gothic-toned and extensive poetry collection *Darkverse: The Shadow Hours* was nominated for the 2018 Elgin Award, while individual poems have been nominated for Rhysling Awards. Stories and verse appear in numerous publications. Other titles include *The Dark Mister Snark, Leery Lane, Odds & Ends, The room at the end of the hall, Cryptic Consequences,* and *An Ill Wind Blows.*

Simon MacCulloch lives in London and writes poetry for a variety of print and online journals, including *Reach Poetry, Black Petals, The Horror Zine, Pulsebeat Poetry Journal, View from Atlantis,* and others.

J. G. Maybrook is a writer and librarian based in Upstate New York. He has contributed to a variety of small press publications, and his work includes stories, essays, and poems. When he is not writing or at work at the library, he enjoys walking in the countryside and gardening with his wife Hannah.

Michael Minassian is a contributing editor for *Verse-Virtual,* an online poetry journal. His poetry collections *Time Is Not a River, Morning Calm,* and *A Matter of Timing* as well as a chapbook, *Jack Pays a Visit,* are all available on Amazon.

Ngo Binh Anh Khoa is a teacher of English in Ho Chi Minh City, Vietnam. In his free time, he enjoys daydreaming, reading, and occasionally writing poetry for personal entertainment. His speculative poems have appeared in NewMyths.com, *Heroic Fantasy Quarterly, The Audient Void,* and other venues.

Manuel Pérez-Campos's poetry has appeared previously in *Spectral Realms* and *Weird Fiction Review*. A collection of his poetry in the key of the weird is in progress; so is a collection of ground-breaking essays on H. P. Lovecraft. He lives in Bayamón, Puerto Rico.

Jack Ranieri is a student at the Los Angeles Film School. Professionally he is a working stiff and is always an amateur level of adult navigating life from Syracuse, New York.

Geoffrey Reiter is Associate Professor and Coordinator of Literature at Lancaster Bible College. He is also an Associate Editor at the website *Christ and Pop Culture*, where he frequently writes about weird horror and dark fantasy. As a scholar of weird fiction, Reiter has published academic articles on such authors as Arthur Machen, Bram Stoker, Clark Ashton Smith, and William Peter Blatty. His poetry has previously appeared in *Spectral Realms* and *Star*Line*, and his fiction has appeared in *Penumbra* and *The Mythic Circle*.

Jessica Amanda Salmonson is the author of the heroic fantasy trilogy *The Tomoe Gozen Saga* and the nonfiction work *The Encyclopedia of Amazons*. Her short story collections include *A Silver Thread of Madness* and *The Deep Museum: Ghost Stories of a Melancholic*. Her poetry has appeared in a Rhysing Awards anthology and in Ellen Datlow and Terri Windling's *The Year's Best Fantasy and Horror*.

David Schembri is an award-nominated author, artist, comic creator and poet from Australia. He is the author of *Unearthly Fables* (The Writing Show, 2013), *Beneath the Ferny Tree* (Close-Up Books, 2018), and the comics, *Splitting Sides: Tales of Humorous Horror #1 & #2,* and *Crowman #1*. His first novella was released in 2024 by Odyssey Books. David's short fiction has been published by Chaosium Inc, Horror World Press, Things in the Well, Black Beacon Books and Midnight Echo. His poetry has been published in *Spectral Realms*, *Midnight Echo*, *Silver Blade Magazine*, and anthologies by *Rainfall Books*.

Ann K. Schwader lives and writes in Colorado. Her newest collection, Unquiet Stars, is now out from Weird House Press. Two of her earlier collections, *Wild Hunt of the Stars* (Sam's Dot, 2010) and *Dark Energies* (P'rea Press, 2015), were Bram Stoker Award Finalists. In 2018, she received the Science Fiction and Fantasy Poetry Association's Grand Master award. She is also a two-time Rhysling Award winner.

Darrell Schweitzer has been publishing weird or fantastic poetry for decades. Not counting comic verse (e.g., *They Never Found the Head: Poems of Sentiment and Reflection*, 2001) his two previous collections of (mostly weird) verse are *Groping Toward the Light* (2000) and *Ghosts of Past and Future* (2008). Hippocampus Press will issue a new volume of previously uncollected and selected poems, *Dancing Before Azathoth*, in 2025. His most recent story collection is *The Children of Chorazin* (Hippocampus Press, 2023) and his most recent anthology is *Weird Tales: The Best of the 1920s* (Centipede Press, 2025).

John Shirley won the Bram Stoker Award for his book *Black Butterflies: A Flock on the Dark Side*. His first poetry collection, *The Voice of the Burning House,* has been nominated for the Elgin Award for poetry.

Oliver Smith is an artist and writer from Cheltenham, Gloucestershire, UK. His poetry has appeared in *Dreams & Nightmares, Eye to the Telescope, Illumen, Mirror Dance, Rivet, Spectral Realms, Star*Line,* and *Weirdbook.* His collection of stories, *Stars Beneath the Ships,* was published by Ex Occidente Press in 2017, and many of his previously anthologized stories and poems are collected in *Basilisk Soup and Other Fantasies.* Smith is studying for a Ph.D. in Creative Writing.

DJ Tyrer is the person behind Atlantean Publishing and has been published in *The Rhysling Anthology,* issues of *Cyäegha, The Horrorzine, Scifaikuest, Sirens Call, Star*Line, Tigershark,* and *The Yellow Zine.* The e-chapbook *One Vision* is available from Tigershark Publishing. *SuperTrump* and *A Wuhan Whodunnit* are available for download from Atlantean Publishing.

Yuliia Vereta is a Polish writer of Ukrainian origin who is now living her third life in Katowice, where she works as a translator. Her speculative works have been published in print and online, among others in *Star*Line, Dreams and Nightmares, Asimov's Science Fiction, Leading Edge, Penumbric, Kaleidotrope*, and *ParSec*. She is a 2022 Best of the Net nominee.

Steve Vertlieb has been writing about films, and the history of "Music for the Movies," in books, magazines, journals, and online for over half a century. He is the recipient of the "Rondo Hall of Fame" Lifetime Achievement Award, joining previous recipients Ray Bradbury, Ray Harryhausen, Christopher Lee, Peter Cushing, and Robert Bloch.

Andrew White lives in the mountains of North Carolina, where he jots down a poem from time to time. He derives inspiration from the mystical, the mythological, and all things Gothic/Lovecraftian. Andrew loves nature, his family, and black metal. A handful of his poems have been published, mostly in *Spectral Realms.*

Steven Withrow has written three chapbooks—*The Sun Ships, The Bedlam Philharmonic*, and *The Nothing Box*—and a collaborative collection, *The Exorcised Lyric* (with Frank Coffman). His speculative and dark fantasy poems have appeared in *Asimov's, Spectral Realms, Space & Time*, and *Dreams & Nightmares*. His work was nominated for the Rhysling and Elgin awards, and he wrote the libretto for a chamber opera based on a classic English ghost story. He lives on Cape Cod.

Lee Clark Zumpe, an entertainment editor with Tampa Bay Newspapers, earned his bachelor's degree in English at the University of South Florida. He began writing poetry and fiction in the early 1990s. His work has regularly appeared in a variety of literary journals and genre magazines over the last few decades.

www.ingramcontent.com/pod-product-compliance
Lightning Source LLC
Chambersburg PA
CBHW060807050426
42449CB00008B/1586